3X

By

Jermar Jerome Smith

INTRO

First I want to thank someone special who I have no shame as to admitting without them who knows where many of my short ideas would be. Esther without her committed advising and subtle manipulation as to creating a children's book for her I wouldn't have had the devotion or spirit as to make this short project a reality in front of you today. Ideas are never a issue for me but putting things down the way I see them is definitely a challenge, but I guess it is for artist I bet. So it's a must I thank her for all her encouragement and consistency in urging me to have uplifted spirits and positive centered feelings in anything I do at all times. YOU ARE APPRECIATED.

anthology [an-thol-uh-gee]

Why ANTHOLOGY ? Some may ask this question and my answer
comes as simple as anything. It comes only from my love for anthology
series and films. Seriously every sense I was little some of my favorite
films to watch early on was "Creepshow", The Outer Limits, "Tales
From the Darkside" the movie (loved the series later), and my most
favorite of them all was and is one of my top favorite television series of
all time that I even heard is being rebooted (pray that it isn't). Tales from
the MUTHAFUCKIN Crypt. I loved that show so much I would stay up
until 10 and 10:30 just to see it on regular t.v. every Saturday night
faithfully. I mean I was a baby I'm talking five and six years old looking
at this gory horror and sexually explicit show at night all by myself (but
I saw worst) wasn't too long after when my dad even took me and my
sister to see it's feature film debut because the crypt keeper got so big
because of the shows loyal viewers, I guess the Hollywood studio's felt
cool green lighting a off shoot movie that became a cult classic called
"Demon Knight ". Man when it dropped I remember vividly the entire
theatre packed with people standing up just to see it. Same thing with
"Tales From the Hood " also a anthology inspiration and even now one
of my top films of all time based on subject matter and much love to the
brotha Rusty Cundieff for creating it. Shit I even remember Cat's Eye
with then young Drew Barrymore, written by it's dubbed king the
master of horror himself Stephen King. As I grew the love of segment
features didn't die down by twenty-three I had been collected all Tales
from the crypt seasons on dvd and the same with Tales from the
Darkside. I even got serious with the Twilight Zone and it's reboot series
in the 80's, it's modern version which I remember distinctly too that
came out in the 2000's that was hosted by Forest Whittaker was a
favorite. Is now on my purchase radar and I'll soon make apart of my
collection when the time is right.

Now even though those classics drove in the genre of horror I went a different direction with my tales and told them from a perspective that will soon become a seasoned topic on my readers ears. And will for sure make my mark in book savvy and creativity as a writer. YOU WATCH ! In the meantime I thought I lend some back story on crafting this new inception and putting it out before the world. Along with the several historical classics I owe conceiving this book to the list of numerous anthology films and television series I couldn't help mentioning that I enjoyed from a child until now a grown man. On that behalf I want to say, good looking and this embracing is FROM ME to YOU. ENJOY !

CONTENTS

NA NA'S LITTLE SECRET

I remember on January days like this that I would spend with my grandmother Na Na outside her backyard. I was only six years old and more than toys, t.v., or even reading my book. I always loved to help my grandmother plants all types of seeds to grow in her garden she named Kemit. Kemit was more than a garden it was a palace imaged to me at that time like a football field how big I thought it was. Regardless how I pictured Kemit, there wasn't any pig skin tossing, touchdown running, head up tackling circulating in any parts to these confines. It was only one kind of thing that roam this turf and had its purpose and that was Na Na's famous produce. That filled the area in bunches and patches that some and even I as a small child couldn't imagine. Staring before this produce forest type that had all types of fruits and vegetables all around this backyard. Recollecting now I can remember where everything was placed at exactly. From the scrumptious carrots, vital beets, craving cabbage, soul sage, superb squash, plump potatoes, trusty tea, and blazing onions that was potent enough to cure a pain. On the left side of Kemit to leave a feel and taste for you. While her wonderful walnuts filled with nutrients, juicy watermelon, vine ripe tomatoes, plump strawberries, or jamming blackberries don't even get me started with her orange tree that thirst her household every morning fresh squeezed for breakfast. Or the lemon one far to the back near her kale and watercress bloom that on summer days kept my black piggy bank filled to the limit with all sorts of quarters, nickels, and dimes when she prepped me to go out to the curb for selling.

Just about everyone within radius in our town knew about Na Na's garden. Caught such a big buzz that she allowed people three days out of the year to come through at scheduled times that I was more than pleased to assist in phone calls. To come from all over to view or purchase her magic incarnate. I remember clear as day my dad posting a sign above the fence near the fruit trees that had the banner "Na Na's Little Secret". The words were scribbled in blue and pink marker with the very same color scheme traced with Christmas tree lighting bulbs around them. It was a sight to see, that you really had to be there to witness. All the fuss around in the town was due to my beloved grandmother and her luxurious produce spread in her backyard that was all the talk. People would say was she was the lady that grew produce even better than the grocery stores and markets. And you didn't have to worry about any dangerous pesticides or chemicals being added, Na Na's was all natural.

Almost to point where her inventory was labeled to being mystifying and possessing great powers into healing folks. A woman a few counties over who worked in the newspaper actually printed that in a page column she wrote for after claiming Na Na's cabbage and kale cured her of alopecia that was hereditary. A few weeks later she posted another story where a man also made a account stating after consuming tea from kemit the odd and itchy rash he had that not even doctors were sure to diagnose as had suddenly by some strange luck dissolved. The lady came up and paid tribute to my grandmother by just getting a picture with her and thanking her in great sincerity. Na Na welcomed her in open arms and graced a great big smile on her face as she snapped a photo of all three of us standing in kemit before serving her a helping of freshly made sweet potato pie from scratch compliments from you know who (Kemit itself).

Like it being all natural, her goods was also most importantly all hers. She had sole control of all ownership the way she wanted, no partners, loaners, or most deceiving the all see eye watching, meaning the corporations. But it didn't stop them from trying. Once March with the picture had left, April soon brought more visitors and not the kind appreciative in health and beauty that kemit displayed. Oh sure they claim to be admirers at first but that was the hook they bait you in for what Na Na called "long-term investment" that was the sinker. Many multi billion corporations make they're entire living off of other people's ideas and gifts. See what they do is, discover you and see the profitable market and base you have at a local level. Then scheme you on the more money you can make and missing out on every second of the day. If and only if you sign deals with them where you do all the work, they put out your product all over, make majority of the profit and then front you a small portion of it. Then call it business.

They couldn't sell on that scheme though, not here, not now, so long as Na Na had anything to do about it. She saw them coming miles away and wouldn't jeopardize her love and hobby for riches at all. All was left when they came she would send the gentlemen with his white shoes, and white suit on his merry way declining his offer without even a thought. They came again in June with the same interest but beholding a different proposal this time.

He knocked on the door and Na Na sat the man down in the living room and she didn't even offer him a drink I recalled. Even though his name escapes me but the situation and conversation didn't. This man claimed to be of a very important agency within the United states he said while he stared at me with a smile I only return with a cold look having seen grandma doing the same. He had heard about the paper and the article and wanted her permission in sampling one of the products mentioned in it. Stating the contents may can be of use to healing the world and can be very profitable for her if she agreed to the allocation. Saying his intentions was strictly in saving lives and even went as far as to doing all he could as to trying coerce Na Na into making the same plea. That beautiful woman though was too intellectually stubborn, she wouldn't have it. She declined the same and escorted the man out of the house with his hopes and dreams he schemed in his back pocket now mushed to the living room floor.

I mean even I could see through what he truly wanted with all his codes words and gestures the same as the dude before. When he was gone I got the courage to ask her.

- Na Na, why didn't you want to be a millionaire like the man wanted to make you ?

I asked.

- Because baby girl, not everything is for sale, when you get older you'll see that some things. Are best kept secret.

Gracing a smile on her face.

Once the summer had left, the fall came which meant a new harvest for Kemit. Good thing because the old had nearly dried up with sales, giveaways, and guilty pleasures by me my time spent at Na Na's on the regular. The new harvest meant fresh squash, corn, beans, peanuts, and all sorts of other goodness. I remember it falling on a October that we brought it in, my mom and dad helped when they could. I made it my mission straight from school too. On one day when we were finished for the day and Na Na had food on the stove. She got a knock on the door just before the moon came out. She opened the door and a man this time more well suited almost conservative approached and he didn't brush a smile behind his blue eyes. He held a briefcase after calling grandma by her full name that was rare to hear. Then did something I've never even saw someone visiting do. Offer himself inside instead of awaiting Na Na to ask. Finally she agreed and he sat down in the living room dreading his visit called for urgent notice. He made his message short and sweet I could tell he was refrained as I came in he was removed from gracing gentle spirits opposed to the others.

- Ms. Darling unfortunately I have no better way in saying this but your property has been chosen. And you have a deadline to four months to determine your decision within this sudden understanding.

The blue eyed man said.

But Na Na was and always will be, never to back down from anyone no matter what the cause or circumstance. No pleas, cries, or begging for them to reconsider. She'd never allow anyone that satisfaction, so she just stood there and laughed him off while his eyes stay concerned on her. Awaiting a response but she only gave him only one opening and it was to the front door then waving her hand to the outside showing him out. Then slammed the door behind him, pulled her arm comfortably around my shoulder and went right back in the kitchen to return cooking. I loved that lady. Making it the third offer she denied, made me question later how many would there be especially now that the new crop had just came. People even started as to calling earlier before Na Na made it known that kemit would have its opening the same as every year.

Not in a million years I thought what happened even could happen. But it did. It started with after the harvest and December came in for the winter and a bad smell sprang over kemit. It was terrible, the worst stench you could ever come across. A mystery to Na Na as to what it was even when she called a expert to try it out, but yet still even he couldn't riddle the smell. Days later it got worst climbing from the garden and now into the house, and it got so bad that Na Na no longer wanted me over anymore because it was giving me nausea bad that I missed a few days of school. And in a couple weeks I didn't hear from her and when I did there wasn't any good news. My mom told me she had caught a fever and had to be cling to bed rest at a nearby hospital.

We went to visit and I saw her on the bed and couldn't believe that this strong woman who I loved looked the way she did so fast. It was only three weeks later and Na Na had looked terribly weak and without rest. I went to her as she called and she told me what was next and tears fell down my face. I would never forget what she told me, she asked if I could keep a secret. Always I said, she called for me to come closer as she whispered into my ear. Then asked me after could I keep it and of course I promised. She smiled one last time for me before we had to go, and to this day that vision of her is stuck hold to my mind like glue even now as I speak about it. She died the following night, new years eve. It was last day of December.

After the funeral not more than two weeks had moved on and Na Na's house of course was willed in our favor so as kemit. A day later I saw my mother with my father explaining a letter that she had received in the mail that explained the seizure that I had already knew. Animals they were, the old woman of beauty hadn't even been gone a month. Her spirit was probably still here and yet they're only concern was persistence in what was her prize love. Unlucky to them though a few days later that old house would no longer stand after we heard it went up in flames until every piece of it was ash, and the beloved famous garden had withered in rot from the awful scent we speculated.

For a long time and over the years that one single year would always stick with me and never could go anywhere. To me having that last time with Na Na and kemit was more than a memory, it was a lifetime of love. I've had many others as I ascended into a now woman but nothing can compare. Whenever I start to think about Na Na she wasn't hard to see. Above our mantle in a ancient vase encrypted with beautiful designs that resonated Nile valley culture in great uniqueness. After college I left home on a trip and visited the place that was once called kemit and made a land for myself. A house, a backyard, and a garden that stretched over the sphinx's horizon that reign high in gold beauty once the sun shined and then set. Almost the same as Na Na's was that I could remember when I was girl. When I got the chance and my first harvest came into being, I made a call home and sent for one thing that was missing. And when it came marked in those sharp ancient designs spirited in Egyptian pattern with great uniqueness. There standing on the land with my produce beauty adjacent to kemit as the sun came in with the smell of fresh fruit and vegetable hanging aromatic strong to the minor breeze. It was there I open the urn vase and released her... see I told Na Na I'd keep her little secret.

NANA : Ghanaian name meaning "mother of the Earth."

IS IT WORTH IT ?

IS IT WORTH IT ?

Martinique at only 12 years old has a ability mastered that many her age just aren't mentally capable of doing or at the rate she dwells. While her teacher scribbling mind intimidating equations on the board that most children at her age cant fathom to devise a answer to. Leaping her hand in the sky she has no trouble in doing so at the center of her classroom attention as she's called on and does the unspeakable cracking open the arithmetic's case with ease as if it all comes to her so organic like apart of her DNA. But routine curriculum agendas aren't the only overwhelm Martinique has to her student file in academic excel, along with her 4.0 GPA. She also in her age bracket scored higher than any other child in the county on the culturally bias standardized tests at only ten and eleven years old.

This year she in order to prove certain figures who uphold the test wrong, instructors along with her school's principal came up with the idea since denying the young brain wiz to advance classes. She was option by the board of education along with thousands of petition signers to have her take the high school's version. In which she blew out of waters. Making Martinique Harriet Rivers a household name throughout the entire area.

If there's anyone deemed for success at any standard it's her. However more times we as people care to acknowledge having great promise isn't a deterrent to one's issue, or a savior to their personality. To Martinique the classroom is one world while outside of it be another. And outside is a place where she strides in excellence as well only from a different perspective, a view more catering to negativity in anyway fit. Lying, cheating, and most pleasurable to her is thieving.

Don't be fooled by her age, as skilled as she is in education she's just the same in stealing. A few years earlier Martinique stole just about anything she came across. You name it she swiped it. Candy, lip gloss, money, jewelry, she stole anything if it was in a store she took it, kept it, while most times she sold it discount to friends at school. It escalated little than a year ago where she came across a popular shirt in a store that she just couldn't see herself not having. Getting away with it she became a natural crook and it got her intrigued more and more, but not in comparison to a child, her game was a bit more above the ordinary.

What she'd do is after school she take a bus to a mall she had planned ahead of time and wander into store after store she could and find something she'd want, take it, but pay for something minor or small that'll never suspect her presence. Like a nail polish or bracelet. And every time it worked, leaving no one not as so much a squint in her direction.

She had numerous swipe methods to choose from being that the behavior had became a second profession and her mind a track field in creative thought tactics to use. Whether it be 'Sleevin' a maneuver where you tuck a small shirt or top into the sleeve of something you had on. But it required a jacket, the heavier the better. Or 'Slippin' where you pack a pair of pants or jeans from inside to the back of your hoody or jacket which required a filled book bag, because it held the item in place behind you and unseen.

Then last which is her favorite but only used for specific items that aren't easy to lift. Like coats, jackets, or maybe shoes it's called 'Slidin'. 'Slidin' is picking items up one by one naturally carefully keeping ordinary shopping composure until gathering enough clothes to a big bunch then racing to the dressing room to try on. That's the bait, your not trying on clothes your grabbing that one big bad piece that you wouldn't usually steal that goes into your book bag without the censor. Pick the cheapest thing you'd picked up in the bunch. Out the dresser room in fifteen minutes, then you carefully return every other item back in its place before copping the decoy shirt or pants. When your done "Thank you", "Goodbye", "have pleasant evening" and your gone, business as usual. Not on this day, not in this store, this mission wouldn't be so sweet for meddling Martinique.

It started as when she stepped into this store like all the others and worked her way easy pass the female cashier and began her stages to 'Slidin'. She got about five items (including a coat) and found herself into the dressing room before it was all over that's where she made her move. It only took a few minutes and she was out and back in position. Placing every piece back into its original place. When finished she paced to the register where she held up a shirt to the cashier in confidence and gladly handed the mature woman the total. The lady wraps up the service and hands Martinique the bag as she begins to stroll out the door before these words escape the cashier's lips that she didn't see it coming from a mile away.

- Is it worth it ?

She asks.

- Is what ?

- The jacket...is it worth that much to steal.

- Steal ? I did steal anything.

- Ok ! So it's fine if I ask you to open up your book bag right now before I close and lock my entrance door automatically.

At the flick of a switch on the wall beside the register she does so. The door shuts close and you can hear the bolts click into place as it locks with only those two inside.

- Uh oh ! I know that look. You thinking you should of ran when I said steal, huh.

She laughs.

Martinique swiping spree has now met a crossroad.

The cashier taking her to the back, empties out her book bag with the coat and a few other shirts she had picked up from a few other stores before entering hers. The lady even picks up some costume jewelry out of her jacket pocket and some jeans she had slipped. Then lays out all the items Martinique had stolen over a table for her to see. It had to been over ten pieces she had stolen just that day. Most of it was top of the line gear. Shirts, pants, miscellaneous, and the coat ranging between at least seven hundred dollars.

- There's at least six to seven hundred dollars worth of stuff here. Now I'm going to give you a way out. You can call me Mrs. Green and if you confess your parents number I can guarantee there won't be any police involved.

- The precise estimation is seven hundred and ninety-six dollars and twelve cents. You can check for your self with that calculator over there if you want.

She replies. The cashier turns to calculator after intrigue to her proper estimation.

- You look familiar ? What is your name ? How old are you ?

She asks. But Martinique resists in reply.

- Ok...fine you leaving in handcuffs out my store is your parents problem having a thief for a child is their situation not mines.

Dialing nine, one, one in attempt to scare.

- Alright...my name is Martinique Rivers. I'm twelve.

- Martinique Rivers...The smart girl, wait what are your parents number ?

She asks. While Martinique hesitates again in answering, there's a long pause between them as she just sits there jittering as tears begin to stream down her cheeks from her eyes. Again the cashier lady asks confused.

- Where is your mother or father ? Pick one. I don't care.

She tells. Finally she's has enough, she tried and tried but no longer can hold it in.

- I DON'T HAVE ANY FUCKING PARENTS.

And although her other side was habit in producing lies. This wasn't one of them at all. Martinique's rebellious conduct wasn't seasoned out of thrill but more to survival which is why she took to stealing and more times selling the stuff she stole for cash. Her only home was a local group with other girls just like her or worst, all spaced in a cramped house. It took some convincing but the lady cashier stayed with Martinique in the back of that shop room until she told her everything. No police were called, in fact no one was throughout their whole conversation. The woman only asked for a apology and wanted

Martinique to make a serious commitment as to vowing to never steal anything ever again...and she did right there. Ten years passed. And in a store Martinique does a interview behind a register counter with a local media personality . The host doesn't hold back in asking any questions. Whether it be in discussing topics as entrepreneurial, school, and her future. Martinique doesn't shy away from answering but the most interesting question of all the host asks standouts to her.

- With everything you know and conquered to this point, having a following, inspiring millions of other young black woman and in general like yourself. Who is the one person in your eyes you feel without them you wouldn't know where you'd be up until this point. Who is that person ? What is his or her name ?

- I've never been asked that question and it really is good I have to say. Because that person without a doubt I feel in pertains to your question is a woman by the name of Star Green. Without her none of this would be a reality for me. Not my three stores or my degrees. I definitely know had I not met this woman the way that I did. I wouldn't d be here and most certainly wouldn't have then compassion and integrity that I have now.

Drawn away from the conversation Martinique eye is caught to a young woman with clothes in her hand and a book bag on her back as she then enters into the dressing room

- She's the lady that adopted you, correct.

The interviewer asks.

- Yes, she is.

She replies upon distraction.

When she notices her leaving the room. She sees her put back every piece of clothing she tried on back into its rightful place in de ja vu before approaching the counter to pay. Before the girl leaves, Martinique sees her uniform under her coat, and briefly in a pleasant way tells the interview to wait a moment while she asks the girl who looks her in the eye just before she exits.

- Hey...

- Yes ?

She replies stopping then facing her

- ...is it worth it ?

"According to the United Nations Children's Fund (UNICEF) there are more than 140 million children who are orphans since April 2016."

And no doubt millions more.

With that statistic. How many you think could make a difference in the world if giving chance all like in this story.

MORE THAN THAT

For as long as Aakar could remember since the day he was born his lifelong dream to become as an adult even as young child was to be a police officer. When a toddler his most favorite toy that he was attached to was his remote control police squad cruiser car that made all kinds of alarm and siren noises by button. By the time he could walk and play with the other kids while they wanted to be robbers, he'd most desperately and every time would be the cop happily. Looking for every moment to pull out his plastic cuffs with his plastic little gold badge at the corner of his chest on his shirt and arrest any robber in sight. By ten when he was in school many of his classmates would doodle pictures of they're career path they plan to pursue as they get older. You had some that wanted to be doctors, judges, basketball players, football players, film directors, or artists. Not Aakar, those labels were nothing in his direction into conquering whatsoever, you guessed what he wanted. It was the squad car with the sirens on top, the name badge below his shield he had raised his right hand for while swearing his life to protect and serve every soul he came across while on duty at all times. The blue uniform, the steel metal cuffs, the standard issue piece at his utility belt by his waist, the solidarity between his fellow officers, the look of gaining all walks of life respect once he came upon the public. There was nothing he wanted to do other than be none other than a good ol'boy in blue.

And it didn't make a difference of what anyone thought either. He heard all in routine when it came upon or he brought up over and over amongst peers and family. When he told his mom he wanted to be a cop she say like the rest " You don't wanna do that ", when he told his dad that he wanted to join the force when he became of age his dad would too say "You don't wanna do that", or his friends he grew up with as played outside together and enhanced from games like cops and robbers they also would bestow the same message in fact in more disgust stating it the same "You don't wanna do that ". Even the one person who you would think encourage a child hold heartily and stand in defense against criticism as to him wanting to become whatever he wants in life, his teacher, would again in no hesitation tell Aakar the same exact thing as all his other love ones did. Informing him with great passion with the same format and words that rolled off the others tongue the same as well. "YOU DON'T WANNA DO THAT".

But Aakar didn't care, time moved on and as time came and evolved much older from a boy into almost a full grown man. It was his senior year, seventeen years old when he set it out in plan that by eighteen he would finally live out his dream and nothing would stop him. And no one could except himself.

It happened one night when him and his friends came back from a farewell get together in his brand new first car his dad gifted to him having just completed graduation. A clean classic 1998 Lexus LS400 pearl white that looked to just came off the assembly line. Big enough to turn any head male or female and just so happened to be irresistible by a badge in his cruiser who spotted it a few blocks away from his home.

The cop sweated him and his friends from top to bottom especially about his car, one by one, and then pulled them to the curb handcuffed aided by more than three more badges. While they illegally searched his vehicle, regardless him possessing and displaying his license, registration, and insurance. Aakar couldn't help to the disgusting feeling and experience while him and his friends be profiled while one of the cops look over at him in smile at his inferior position. Knowing there was nothing as a excuse to pull them over. Things got even worst as Aakar tried to explain while his friends pleaded to him to sit still, not say anything, or move from the curb and mention that he was in fact a pupil of a certain recruiter at the precinct while his friends pleaded more in whispers again for him to sit still, not say anything, or move from the curb. He takes their advice, while his only thoughts begin to race about how a few days earlier he was being prepped by a officer to take the test once his birthday arrived in a month. The only thing that lasted in his brain that he remembered was the look of the entire police staff when he entered the precinct, they're widespread look of disgust combined in surprise on each face and one being familiar more than the others as Aakar made his presence subtlety known. After his memory phase the lead cop who is the familiar face the cop turned to him and whip his pistol out and pointed it directly at Aakar's head then stands over him until the search is over.

Aakar couldn't believe it, he saw the gun and in the same instance a car filled with girls he knew look on at him driving slow. Feeling pity but removed from engaging. When it was over that entire night that's all he could think about like it was a nightmare without him in a dream state. The moment did one thing for long as he lived. His days and aspirations to serve as a police were officially broken, spilled, and burnt to a crisp. Aakar wanted nothing to do with that force, instead he studied, read, and observed his surroundings day in and day out from all aspects of his neighborhood. Businesses, schools, streets, young people, and old. Everywhere he turned he saw the police no longer as a influence or resource for the community in protection but more as an tamer or overseer.

It was then he came up with a idea as to not being a threat to community as the police were but more of a assistant to it as it thrived within him. He started up small, first building relationships with each world that had an imbalance, the new not respecting the old and in vice versa. Then bridging them together in social events he threw, making it community oriented. As the events progressed he began to see results, no arguments, no fights, and the threat of all with gunplay. He even had other young men in a few dozen along with friends that followed his template. His functions blossomed away the disunity and transformed it simply to the more loving term as "unity". Aakar went as so far to creating a brand to his work that was in relations to the community that he called "VOCS" defining VANGUARD OF COMMUNITY.

Sensing and realizing his attempts to improve many of the badges got known to his workings by his countless fliers littered all over that you could snatch a shriveled one from off the ground almost anywhere. Enraged, they formed and set a day for his final before the world and all can see.

The day was usual and according to Aakar's everyday normal task handling, eating breakfast. Then patrolling the neighborhood with compatriots, helping young kids across the street and to school, then it's off into the afternoon where he prided in helping local owned business maintain no hassle or harassment from trouble seekers. Responding to any problems when called that grew in very few over time. Before the day was over he all by himself would crossover to a few other nearby communities to spread fliers to future functions at a strip with unknown eyes on him. In no time feeling he was vulnerable coasting up the street, it's where the badges felt the opportunity to strike.

Out one badge jumped from his cruiser and proceeded to stop Aakar and frisk him heavily as he asked why repeatedly. Up against a bus stop portal another cop joins and spread his legs far and wide thoroughly skimming hands all over him. Aakar calls out the oppression while a mini crowd sees from a far and questions begin to assemble and the people form in group as they proceed as one in Aakar's favor. Meanwhile one of the cops goes to his car and removes a handkerchief concealed and begins to plant it on the ground, Aakar sees the move. The people move in and inciting questions to the accosting. The people wish to know why is he's being detained while the other cop tries to restrain the man while the other calls for the crowd that collects more people to disperse immediately even though they resist his orders. Still struggling with Aakar the cop gets frantic and agitated and whips out his gun and pushes it to the back of his head to enforce he's in control and to halt Aakar to stop fidgeting and comply while he goes for his cuffs. This same action excites the cop toward the crowd to do the same as everything turns quiet at once. And I mean everything, the cop attentive to the crowd then advises one last time with kill in his eye for the masses to depart the scene while Aakar is arrested for littering and possessing a unlawful handgun, up in arms if anyone decides different can be labeled a threat and allow the cop to protect himself in his state of fear and outnumbering (Stand Your Ground).

But people never move, even staring down at his standard issue pointed directly at them, one man ahead in the front before the cop states loud and clear.

- You kill him, then you better kill me too.

A woman beside him, steps up and recites the same.

- And after you kill him you better kill me because I'm not going anywhere until you let Aakar go.

A younger boy does the same.

- The same goes for me.

Aakar sees and stares down the little boy who looks over at him while Aakar signals him by nod.

Others say the same while Aakar breaks release the restraint of the other officer on him and turns to look him directly in the eye even while he still points that gun in his midsection. Then slowly he steadies in stride ahead of the crowd staring down the other cop's gun in his face while the other is at his stomach.

- Don't point a gun at a man unless you intend on using it...

- ...and if you intend on using it, you better have enough bullets for all of his friends by him too. How many rounds you think in that nine millimeter Aakar.

- fifteen rounds each...

- So between the two of you, after those rounds go off, let's see how quick you are when it is to getting back five or six steps to that cruiser...if your able to make it. When the crowd behind us gets bigger.

One of the men says.

The two officers still up in arms at Aakar look on as the crowd grows with more people assembling from everywhere. Even one spots a youngster holding a brick menacing in his eyes. Another with a rock. Then a knife and a lead pipe.

More cruisers surface but the two badges already seem to invest in retreating having lowered their weapons on Aakar. They then alert the others before disbanding out. The massive crowd looks on and celebrate in cheer once they see the police are no longer in sight.

They know this won't be the last standoff but forcing them off in fear of their alignment is only a taste to victory. Aakar is beloved by the crowd while he thanks them for unifying when needed. There's a boy held by his mother into the fold, very young that Aakar sees. Barely enough to talk. The boy calls out at Aakar and calls him a cop. He sees and smiles while heading over to the boy there in his mother's arms and saying to him eye to eye. " No... I'm " MORE THAN THAT. "

"We must forget about trying to do for others before doing that which we have not done for ourselves, which is to establish live unity in our brotherhood. You rise up and yell out in ignorance against yourself when you say that you want unity, love and brotherhood of the nations. Those nations look at you-where disunity is the order of the day and see your dislike of self and kind. You are ignorant and foolish people. Your first desire should be love of self instead of love for those other than of your own. If you do not love your own brother- who is of your flesh and blood- how can other than your own flesh and blood accept your love and brotherhood ? First, love thyself and thy own brother as thyself, and others will love you." – Elijah Muhammad: Message to the black man

THE END

www.ingramcontent.com/pod-product-compliance
Lightning Source LLC
Chambersburg PA
CBHW080537030426
42337CB00023B/4768